I0212243

What Others Are Saying About This Book

Dear Dad,

Thank you for letting me read your new book. I think your book is awesome and very much needed in the marriage community. I give you lots of credit and respect for the book and I could surely tell that God was speaking to you while you were writing. I can't begin to fathom writing a book myself. Congratulations!

I love you,

—*Alan Cummins, Christiansburg, Virginia*

It is always important to understand and follow successful people. Through faith, the power of prayer, and hard work all can be achieved. Keep up the good work.

—*Dr. Clark, Port Orange, Florida*

Anyone considering marriage ought to read this book — with his or her future spouse. Carolyn and I took the right path 54 years ago, and luckily haven't strayed! Temptations are greater today, and the path, alas, is wider!

—*W. Thomas Neal, Manager–GE Retired, Hendersonville, North Carolina*

Somewhere, something incredible is
waiting to be known.

— Carl Sagan

If you have knowledge, let others
light their candles at it. — Fuller

LIFE
IS SEXUALLY
TRANSMITTED

❖ ❖ ❖ ❖ ❖

WHY MARRIAGE IS ALL ABOUT CLEAVING

William A. Cummins

CAI Publishing
Port Orange
Florida

Life Is Sexually Transmitted
Why marriage is all about cleaving

William A. Cummins

Published by CAI Publishing
807 Black Duck Drive
Port Orange, FL 32127-4726, USA.

http://www.cleave2.com
newbook@cleave2.com.
866.740.8812

All rights reserved. No part of this book may be reproduced
or transmitted in any form or by any means, electronic or
mechanical, including photo-copying, recording or by
any information storage and retrieval system
without written permission from the author,
except for the inclusion of brief quotations in a review.

All scripture quotations are taken from the
Authorized King James Version (KJV) 1611.

© 2006 by William A. Cummins

Includes personal stories contributed by friends.

Printed in the United States of America

ISBN-10 Print Edition: 0-9787766-6-6
ISBN-13: 978-0-9787766-6-4

ISBN-10 PDF eBook Edition: 0-9787766-7-4
ISBN-13: 978-0-9787766-7-9

DEDICATION

FOR TEENAGERS THROUGH SENIORS,

both married and unmarried,

this book is dedicated to every one who

has ever thought of getting married,

has enjoyed a happy marriage,

or has failed in a marriage.

The happiness of a man in this life does not consist in the absence but in the mastery of his passions.
— Alfred Lord Tennyson

Therefore to him that knoweth to do good, and doeth it not, to him it is sin. — James 4:17

EPIGRAPH

BASED ON THE FACT THAT MARRIAGE IS CON-
stantly losing ground in this land, it appears that
the whole world is waiting for someone to explain what God meant when He said, **"Therefore
shall a man leave his father and mother, and shall
cleave unto his wife: and they shall be one flesh."**
This book reveals how the word **"cleave"** can
profoundly alter our understanding of this his-
torical precept and imbue everyone with a new
awareness of its significance.

If you would not be forgotten, as soon as you are dead and rotten; either write things worth the reading, or do things worth the writing.   — Benjamin Franklin

ACKNOWLEDGMENTS

I WANT TO EXPRESS THANKS TO MY WIFE, ANN, for her encouragement, patience, and assistance while I was writing this book.

My sincere gratitude goes to the following friends who contributed their personal love stories that enrich the book and make it so meaningful: Carol Chappel, Roberta Taylor, Danielle Morel, Lee Orcutt, Gladys Powers, Jane Warner, and Pam Dailey.

Valuable information (and inspiration) was contributed by Tom Neal, Jeff Sumner, Dr. Clark, and Ruthie Davidson. I especially want to thank a special friend, Peggy Painter, for her careful copy editing and helpful commentary during the completion of the book.

DISCLAIMER

THIS BOOK IS DESIGNED TO PROVIDE INFORMATION on the effect cleaving has on marriage. It is sold with the understanding that the publisher and author are not attempting to redefine the Holy Scriptures. If expert biblical assistance is desired, you should seek the services of a competent theologian.

Every effort has been made to make this book as accurate as possible. However, there may be mistakes, both typographical and in content. The purpose of this book is to educate and inspire. The author and publisher shall have neither liability nor responsibility to any person, directly or indirectly, for any problems or troubles alleged to have been caused by the information in this book.

If you do not wish to be bound by the above, you may return this book to the publisher for a full refund.

CONTENTS

I don't think much of a man who is not
wiser today than he was yesterday.
—Abraham Lincoln

A wise man can see more from the
bottom of a well, than a fool can from
a mountain top.   — Unknown

PREFACE

❖ ❖ ❖ ❖ ❖

THIS BOOK CONTAINS MANY OF MY THOUGHTS, beliefs, and personal experiences about God's divine strategy regarding cleaving, marriage, and sexual expression.

However, before any of these God-related events entered my life a major change took place that carried me through life at a higher level than I ever could have imagined. It was probably the most important lesson I ever learned. It deals with attitude and I would like to share it with you in advance of the main text.

I learned about attitude at the early age of eight when my father said, "Bill, if you keep pouting like that, a bird will land on your lower lip someday and leave a deposit." These words got my attention and he then went on to say, "You can pout better than any of your brothers. Maybe you should do something about that." I was the middle child of five boys, ages four through eleven, and had to admit that what he said was true.

Soon after, I heard the story about a grumpy old man in a small town. He was so mean-tempered that people would cross the street to keep from meeting him. Then one day he suffered a severe injury to his face. The surgeon did not know the old man was grumpy and when he sutured his face, he put a smile on his lips. At first the smile bothered the old man, but he soon grew to like it when strangers greeted him pleasantly and said, "Hello, how are you?" Eventually, he became a happy man with many friends.

My tipping point was learning from this story that a smile was simply a frown turned upside down. That's when I decided to put a smile on my lips using scotch brand tape before going to sleep each night. I guess the tape did its job because in a short time my attitude improved and I started smiling more. To an eight-year-old, it was amazing how differently the world looked through the eyes of a smile.

Smiling soon became a way of life for me because people responded to it in a very positive way. I discovered that my smile could even change the attitude of the people I met.

During my career as a young cowboy entertainer, I often appeared on stage with a beautiful palomino stallion that I had trained to perform. Our shows were widely promoted and the headline on the billboards read, "Smilin' Bill and His Wonder Horse, King." This was quite a tribute to a young lad who had to teach himself how to smile.

This positive attitude carried on through my engineering career as well. At one of my early jobs the owner of the company, who was much older than me, would often stop to chat. One day he smiled at me and said, "Bill, your smile reminds me of a short rhyme that I learned long ago." Then he recited this verse: "Anyone can be happy when the world goes along like a song; but the one who's worthwhile, is the one who can smile, when everything goes dead wrong."

Needless to say, I have thought back to that rhyme many times throughout the years, especially when things seemed to go wrong. It has helped me in my career, with my family, and most of all in my marriages.

My advice to everyone is to rise above the negativity that is holding you back and find a way to start smiling your way through life. You are in control of your smile, which means you are also in control of your attitude.

Smile, even if you don't feel like it because it will brighten your day. You will eventually feel it and so will those around you.

Don't wait! Begin today.

> Everything can be taken from a man but one thing: the last of the human freedoms...to choose one's attitude in any given set of circumstances, to choose one's own way.
> —Viktor Frankl, *Man's Search for Meaning*

INTRODUCTION

❖   ❖   ❖   ❖   ❖

ARE YOU AWARE THAT CLEAVING IS A PREREQUISITE to human sexual activity and the transmission of life? Are you aware that God cleaved man to his wife before he commanded them to engage in sex? We are not human beings going through a temporary marriage experience; we are married people going through a temporary human experience.

These statements are factual and will be confirmed in this book which is based upon verse 24 from the second chapter of Genesis: **"Therefore shall a man leave his father and his mother, and shall cleave unto his wife: and they shall be one flesh."**

First the marriage   …   Then the family

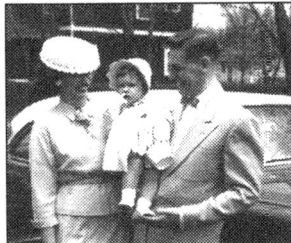

He (Jesus) saith unto them, Moses because of the hardness of your hearts suffered you to put away your wives: but from the beginning it was not so.   —Matthew 19:8

From the beginning, man shall cleave and never leave, and the bride shall be his wife for life.   —William Cummins

PART ONE

WHY MARRIAGE IS ALL ABOUT CLEAVING

❖ ❖ ❖ ❖ ❖

You are about to discover amazing
insights into the dynamics of marriage.
　　　　　　　　—William A. Cummins

CHAPTER ONE

LIFE IS SEXUALLY TRANSMITTED

❖ ❖ ❖ ❖ ❖

WHEN YOU FIRST HEAR SOMEONE SAY, "LIFE IS sexually transmitted" it stops you in your tracks. Sexually transmitted usually brings to mind some type of disease or X-rated thoughts. When you realize what it means, you smile and nod approval. Then, if you are like me, you can't wait to repeat this simple truth to others around you.

When I now observe a lull in a conversation, I loudly proclaim, "Here is something you may not know … life is sexually transmitted!" Then I watch their expressions as they pause, ponder, smile, and finally laugh at this new revelation of truth. We all know in our hearts that sex is a prerequisite for life, but were taught not to discuss it publicly.

If life is sexually transmitted, then God must have a plan in place. During a disquieting period of my life, revealed later in this book, I discovered that a major part of His plan involves cleaving. I was led by the Holy Spirit to Genesis 2:24 in the Old Testament which declares, "Therefore shall a man leave his father and mother, and shall cleave unto his wife: and they shall be one flesh."

Many questions came to mind as I read that verse. "Why use the word **cleave**? What the heck is cleaving? What does it look like? What does it mean? Why is it so important? Why was it positioned in the first book of the Bible?"

Throughout these pages, I plan to answer these questions and in so doing present you with a new way of looking at marriage.

Why Use the Word *Cleave*

Why did God choose this particular word to illustrate the unique bonding of a man and his wife? He could have used words like love, adore, or admire, but He did not. Instead, He chose the word cleave. **Clearly God wanted to speak something into existence that could not be misunderstood.**

He focused on personal intimacy and nailed the door shut on same sex marriage when in the same breath He said, "and they shall be one flesh." One flesh requires combining the DNA of both parents through the birth of a child.

Immediately following their creation, and in a single short verse, God defined the mission of man and woman in His world.

Scriptures such as Ecclesiastes 12:13 which says, "Fear God, and keep his commandments: for this is the whole duty of man" are often used to define man's mission. Although they are useful, they simply reference back to obeying God's intent at the beginning of our creation.

As with all living things, God gave mankind the sexual ability to reproduce its own kind. He

purposefully created man and woman to produce offspring. In Genesis 1:27-28 we read, "So
God created man in his own image, in the
image of God created he him; male and female
created he them. And God blessed them, and
God said unto them, 'Be fruitful, and multiply,
and replenish the earth, and subdue it.'"

Read it again. We were created in God's perfect image, without sin and blessed. Be fruitful
and multiply is **God's first commandment**, and it
requires us to become sexually active. Knowing
this, He fashioned sex to be one of mankind's
greatest pleasures.

Until recent times sex was something to be
awed, a wonderful mystery, a pleasure to be
enjoyed during moments of great intimacy
between a man and a woman. For those who
follow God's plan it is still a life-affirming sensual experience sanctioned by God within the
bonds of marriage.

God knew that holding a marriage together
would not be easy, so He enabled mankind with
enduring spiritual power. I believe when you cut
away all the chaff, man's true nature from the

beginning is spiritual and perfect just like God's true nature.

We are not human beings going through a temporary spiritual experience; we are spiritual beings going through a temporary human experience.

Therefore, when man lives according to his true nature, he is walking with God's power which enables him to carry out his mission. Indeed, God instituted a full partnership with all mankind from the beginning.

Cleaving or Cleavage

My dentist friend said, "I don't know what cleaving is but I do know what cleavage is!" and we all laughed and nodded. Obviously, he was talking about the depression between a woman's breasts especially when made visible by the wearing of a low-cut dress. While cleavage may enhance the mating relationship between men and women it is not beneficial in our dialogue of cleaving.

Cleaving is Altogether another Matter.

To cleave means to divide and penetrate by a cutting blow as when a man leaves his father and his mother. It also means to adhere firmly, closely, loyally and unwaveringly as when a man cleaves unto his wife. Cleaving is then a unique event that bonds two entities together in a very special way.

Cleaving takes on new and extraordinary meaning when God adapts it to marriage. We can understand why a man must leave his father and mother, but what does it mean for him to cleave to his wife?

Can you see a picture of cleaving in your mind? I can see it in mine. Let's take a look at what I see, by opening the windows of our minds.

CHAPTER TWO

A PICTURE OF CLEAVING

❖ ❖ ❖ ❖ ❖

DURING THE FIRST EIGHTEEN YEARS OF MY LIFE, my family heated our house and cooked our food using only firewood. I started splitting firewood when I was strong enough to swing an axe. Follow along as I describe my experiences splitting firewood for our home.

I helped cut down trees on our farm with a cross-cut saw and then trim the trunk and branches into shorter pieces, called rounds, about 15 inches long. To split the pieces into firewood, I would set each round upright on the ground and swing the axe over my head as hard as I could into the top of the round.

The round would normally split along the grain into smaller pieces. Occasionally I would swing my axe into the tree round and instead of splitting, the round would grab hold of the axe head as it sliced part way into it. Vibrations would ring back through the axe handle and penetrate into my hands and arms causing me sharp pain.

When the pain abated, I would try to remove the axe by grasping the handle and lifting the round high in the air. Then I would slam it against the ground again and again, but if the axe head was deeply embedded it could not be shaken free.

Think about it. The axe and round are two separate objects but now they are bonded together. When one object is moved, the other moves with it. Where one goes, the other goes. From now on they are considered a single unit. The axe is now cleaved unto the round. They have become one entity.

I believe the picture on the front cover of this book is God's image of cleaving. The axe is imbedded into the tree round and the round is holding it in a vise-like grip. The axe and the tree round have now become inseparable.

I knew it would take time and energy to remove the cleaved axe head. If I needed to continue chopping, I had to go to the barn for another axe. Later, when I had the time, I would set about removing the cleaved axe from the round.

The only way the axe could be removed was by splitting the round. This was accomplished by placing a steel wedge in front of the axe head and driving it into the round with a sledge hammer. When the round split open, the axe would fall to the ground.

The axe may not be damaged but the tree round would be fractured into pieces. Does this description sound like a typical divorce?

Marriage

As you can see from the book cover image, cleaving is a perfect and wonderful way for God to portray the uniting of a man and a woman in the special union of marriage.

In a Godly marriage the axe represents the husband cleaving unto his wife, with the wife bonding unflinchingly to her husband. From the very beginning, God intended marriage to look like this image.

But this isn't the complete picture. When the Bible describes a Godly marriage we read that a man and his wife are not the only persons involved.

According to the scriptures, two additional entities are necessary to make it work properly. First Corinthians 11:3 records it this way, "But I would have you know, that the head of every man is Christ; and the head of the woman is the man; and the head of Christ is God."

From the beginning, marriage has required a man, his wife, the Christ, and God at the head. When Christ and God are not involved in the marriage we are free to follow our own rules. Consequently we put the marriage in great peril and place ourselves at great risk.

This could be why the Bible describes the marriage relationship immediately after Eve was created. God knew mankind needed to know that its true destiny was to marry and reproduce as succinctly stated in Genesis.

He also knew marriage would be so fragile that mankind should never enter into it without a special kind of bonding. God knew He had to emotionally bind the man and his wife together. To understand God's plan, we must accept and understand that **marriage is all about cleaving.**

Knowing this, we can make the wise choice and invite the power of a loving God into our lives to hold it together through good times and bad.

The strength of cleaving can be illustrated by looking again at the axe embedded in the tree round. If the axe cannot separate from the round by itself, isn't it reasonable to believe that a husband should not purposely leave the marriage union? It logically follows, that in a marriage only death should split the bond and separate the man from his wife.

As we begin to catch a glimpse of what God meant by cleaving, we begin to realize that in His master plan all the elements are in place for a successful marriage relationship. Could our failure to grasp the importance of this crucial event be the beginning of so many unhappy marriages and divorces?

CHAPTER THREE

CHOICES MOLD OUR LIVES

❖ ❖ ❖ ❖ ❖

CLEAVING IS A CHOICE THAT ALTERS THE MEANing of life itself. We often hear that our choices mold our lives. If that is true, how do we go about making the decision to cleave our marriage? What creative process do we follow to make important events like this take place in our lives? Perhaps it will help if we look first at God's creative strategy.

In Genesis 1:3-4 we see this example, "And God said, Let there be light: and there was light. And God saw the light, that it was good:" God followed the same creative process each day. He put His thoughts into words, His words became reality, and then He observed the results. In Geneses 1:31 we read, "And God saw every thing that he had made, and, behold, it was very good." Since we were created in His image, can we follow the same creative process?

Let's look at God's creative strategy again.

His creative process consists of thinking about what He desires, then speaking it into existence, and finally seeing the results. I believe He purposely kept it simple so we could easily adapt it into our personal lives. The big question is; are we able to duplicate His process?

You bet we are!

Our ability to think is the most valuable ability we possess. When we improve the quality of our thinking, we improve the quality of our life. Taking action without thinking first usually leads to failure.

Our whole existence was established on God's own creative process of thinking first, then speaking, and then seeing. How many times have you heard, "You will produce in your experience what you think about and dwell upon" or, "You will become what you think about most of the time"?

The book, "Think and Grow Rich", points out that it is our thoughts that profoundly affect our destiny. It's always interesting to note that the book title does not say, "Work and grow rich" which seems to be the foundation of our entire education system.

The good news is that our thinking actually does produce our lifestyle and relationships. For instance, we cannot do anything for others until we have thought about it first. I believe the golden rule should be changed from, "Do unto others as you would have them do unto you" to, "Think about others as you would have them think about you."

What we think determines what we say, which in turn directs our actions and efforts. Many self help and motivational books have been written about this subject. However, no one put it better than Earl Nightingale, who in the 1950's recorded a life changing message for his business friends called "The Strangest

Secret." I highly recommend that you acquire an audio and follow its suggestions.

Cleaving Requires Total Commitment

Do men and women have a choice of cleaving or not cleaving? The answer is yes, but before reading this book they may not be aware of that choice. With regard to cleaving, it's an assurance sexually or otherwise that is given to each other. It is making a conscious decision to be faithful, no matter what the temptation.

Since cleaving requires total commitments from each other, it also requires that a public ceremony take place to inform the community of their decision. The ceremony announces that they are now bonded together in marriage.

When the husband and wife are totally committed to making their marriage work they are willing to do whatever it takes to enhance each other. Everything they say and everything they do will show their love for each other.

As husband and wife, they enter into a new relationship and must learn to accept each

other's limitations. When they commit to marriage, they should not expect to receive more
from the new relationship than they are willing
to give. This requires dedication to the well-
being of each other, and to the fulfillment of
each others dreams and destinies.

Commitment is not just thinking thoughts
and speaking words; it requires action and time
to make it deep and lasting. It especially
requires a willingness to publicly declare their
unreserved commitment to each other through
a marriage ceremony.

Ultimately, through their marriage, they will
discover who they are as they learn to give
freely of themselves.

Total commitment to marriage also requires
constant affirmation and feedback, even when
they may disagree. They must show the world
that they take each other very seriously by sup-
porting one another. Everyone needs to feel
valuable and connected and, above all, to feel
loved. Through marriage, God fulfills the needs
of the whole family.

God Said to Husbands

In Ephesians 5:25 God insures that the husband is totally committed to his wife. "Husbands, love your wives, even as Christ also loved the church, and gave himself for it." This is reaffirmed in verse 5:28, "So ought men to love their wives as their own bodies. He that loveth his wife loveth himself."

The relationship between a husband and his wife is a holy union in which responsibility is shared. Although the husband is assigned the family leadership role, he is to share in all the duties that are required to make a family function smoothly.

God Said to Wives

In Ephesians 5:22 we read an interesting and often troubling command: "Wives, submit yourselves unto your own husbands, as unto the Lord." We can understand how some wives may be offended by this. But when wives look back at the image of cleaving on the cover, they see that if the tree round had not submitted to the axe, there would be no cleaving. With this image in mind the scripture takes on new meaning and significance.

God Said to Children

In Ephesians 6:1-4 it says: "Children, obey your parents in the Lord: for this is right. Honour thy father and mother; which is the first commandment with a promise; That it may be well with thee, and thou mayest live long on the earth. And, ye fathers, provoke not your children to wrath: but bring them up in the nurture and admonition of the Lord."

The children are blessed when they honor their parents, and the parents honor each other. The greatest gift any father can show his children is his love for their mother, and the greatest gift any wife can show her children is to respect their father. Commitment, respect, love, and honor must all labor together.

What Does It All Mean

There should be no doubt by now that just as our choices determine our personal lives, they also establish the destiny of our marriage. We see how choices affect our lives when we observe how Jesus responded to the needs of His bride, the church.

It is amazing how God continues to use this example to show us a true picture of His relationship with mankind. Just as Jesus chose to love the church and to give His life for her, we can choose to honor our marriage partner.

The greatest lesson we can learn from this example is simply this, "Unselfish love knows no bounds."

CHAPTER FOUR

GOD'S HIDDEN SECRETS

❖ ❖ ❖ ❖ ❖

THE MYSTERIES BEHIND CLEAVING ARE RE-vealed when we clearly picture it in our mind's eye. On the cover of this book we can see the image of cleaving after the woodsman thrusts his axe into the tree round.

We can even picture the woodsman swinging the axe, with our eyes following the blade as it arches downward, cutting into the wood, and suddenly stopping with a shock.

As you study the image, do you notice a couple of things missing? Take another look and if you do not see the unseen, ask yourself, who is the woodsman, and where did he get the energy to swing the axe into the round?

You know the axe did not swing itself, and the woodsman is not revealed. What power exists that could emotionally cleave a man unto his wife? To find the answers you must turn again to the scriptures for an explanation.

Secret No. 1
"God puts His energy into the marriage."

Cleaving would be impossible if God had not spoken it into existence. We must understand that God and His word are one and the same. When I was young my father would say, **"My word is me."** I thought this was a very profound statement. Now I understand it because it is based upon God's nature that is revealed when His thoughts are spoken into reality.

In marriage, God energizes the man and the wife through His word to accept the cleaving and the bonding. The ultimate purpose is one flesh and a fulfilling marriage that will last a life-time. In Genesis 2:24, God moves the man away from his parents and cleaves him unto his wife. With cleaving completed, the marriage is placed under the husband's leadership.

At first glance this arrangement seems unworkable. Then we see the picture change drastically as the woman takes center stage. When they become one flesh, the wife is destined to carry, nurture, and care for the baby. She is the one who now builds a solid family structure.

To do this successfully she must be loved and protected by her husband. In our marriage image, the axe represents the husband. It also symbolizes the husband's essential obligation to build and maintain the home, and to lead and defend the family.

When we understand the unique structure of a Godly marriage, it brings harmony into our lives and into society.

Secret No. 2
"Cleaving takes place during courtship."

The ties that bind a marriage together are the emotional experiences of the lovers' hearts and minds during courtship. Courting makes sense when we understand what God meant by cleaving.

The natural instincts of both sexes are for the man to pursue the woman. Men are aggressive and enjoy the elation of pursuit. Women are alluring and subtle, which is why women glow during the courtship. However, both must play their parts in this drama to make it work successfully.

It takes two to tango, so courtship normally begins with an introduction, followed by small talk, and then mutual attraction. From this point on the chase is underway. It's a mating dance where the man takes the lead and the woman follows. The bonding occurs when they both enjoy the dance and want it to continue.

There are eight love stories included at the end of this book. Though they are different, each reveals that cleaving occurred during courtship and ended in a happy marriage.

The process of cleaving is so natural it fades from memory like an old secret. God surely did not intend for cleaving to be a secret. That's why He put it in the first book of the Bible in the second chapter of Genesis.

Secret No. 3
"God's power is in His word."

Looking back, I can see that every time I faltered, I had taken my eyes off God and tried to live by my own rules. Since God puts His energy into marriage through cleaving, He uses His word to hold it spiritually together.

It took a few years for God to get my attention but I started yielding to His will when I was about 20 years old. Since that time, I've asked for His word every day by following an early-morning prayer routine.

After reciting the Lord's Prayer, which is a true revelation of God the Father, I express my concerns and desires. Then I listen as He converses with my thoughts. This routine can take from a few minutes to over an hour because I don't want to rush through our time together. Then, I ask for His spiritual word to walk on and to sustain me throughout the day ahead. His word arrives in the form of scripture passages and personal messages.

Believing that I was created in God's image, I conclude my prayer routine with this positive affirmation: "Father, I know You are helping me and that all my negative thoughts (including doubt, unbelief, fear, and failure) have no power against me because I claim my own real nature that is spiritual and perfect. Amen."

The four major negative thoughts of Doubt, Unbelief, Fear, and Failure are grouped together because they can exert extreme negative pressure on the spiritual lives of most people. For simplicity I call this group of negative thoughts, "The Duffs."

Why would I seek God's word for the day ahead you may ask? In Ephesians we learn the basic faith walk. God first asks us to sit with Him, then to walk with Him, and finally to stand on His word. My point is simply this: "How do you know what good you should be doing during the day if you don't ask God for His specific guidance every day?"

When we ask God for His word and then walk out on it in faith, we manifest His power directly into our lives. We see a good example when Peter did not have the power to walk on the water until after Jesus said the word, **"Come."** In Matthew 14:27-31, we see this scene unfold:

But straightway Jesus spake unto them, saying, Be of good cheer; it is I; be not afraid. And Peter answered him and said, Lord, if it be thou, bid me come unto thee on the water. And he said, Come. And when Peter was come down out of the ship, he walked on the water, to go to Jesus. But when he saw the wind boisterous, he was afraid; and beginning to sink, he cried, saying, Lord, save me. And immediately Jesus stretched forth his hand, and caught him, and said unto him, O thou of little faith, wherefore didst thou doubt?

The Bible is filled with stories of God's word in action. If we do not walk on God's word, we are walking on our own and that is dangerous. We see Peter begin to sink when he doubted God's word and we may very well do the same.

Of course Satan tries to enter into our prayers to deceive us, so we must learn to evaluate the messages we receive. I suggest you follow the same discernment guidelines that I use:

1. God's word is softly spoken, as a loving Father, and consistent with His nature. His word is based on the spirit of the law and leads to life. In James 1:5 we read: "If any of you lack wisdom, let him ask of God, that giveth to all men liberally, and upbraideth not; and it shall be given him."

Simply ask God for spiritual guidance, and expect Him to reply based on Romans 8:14 which says, "For as many as are led by the Spirit of God, they are the sons of God."

2. Satan is also consistent to his nature. His word is always based on the letter of the law which leads to judgment and death. He is the "accuser of our brethren" (Revelations 12:10) and never speaks mercy, always judgment.

3. You must walk on God's word for a while to get to know His voice. You learn to know the gentle voice of the Good Shepherd through experience, and sometimes by following the wrong voice and learning from mistakes.

I strongly recommend learning the difference between Law and Grace from a gifted teacher, and then becoming a serious student of the Bible. Only then can you withstand the wiles of the devil by putting on the whole armor of God and by exercising all the gifts of the Holy Spirit.

During our lives there are always situations when we do not know the right thing to do. When we can discern God's will for us on a daily basis it takes much of our stress away. Each of us should have our own daily walk with God and each of us can discern His will if we simply seek it with our whole heart.

Of course knowing God's will always carries responsibility along with it. In James 4:17 we read, "Therefore to him that knoweth to do good, and doeth it not, to him it is sin." It certainly gives us great comfort to know what God wants us to do before we do it.

Through my prayers, God has helped me with my two marriages, my family, and my work. Following what I believe to be God's will has worked for me, and I believe it will do the same for you. I highly encourage you to include early-morning prayer in your daily life.

CHAPTER FIVE

THE TURNING POINT

❖ ❖ ❖ ❖ ❖

I'VE ALWAYS MARVELED AT GOD'S WISDOM IN creating man and woman. He first created Adam and then created Eve from the body of Adam. He sexually united them so uniquely that their children were reproduced from the body of Eve. How marvelous!

Cleaving is the picture of a Godly marriage between a man and a woman. It's a special union that leads to fulfillment for the family. The marriage alliance is so special that it should only be separated by death because in the overall scheme of things death is a part of living. See Romans 14:8, "whether we live therefore, or die, we are the Lord's."

My first experience of cleaving was the moment I become totally committed to my first wife. I call this phase of my life "The Turning Point" because it completely changed my life in a very blessed way.

I met Phyllis during work shortly after she graduated from high school. I had previously moved from the farm to a nearby city and was working at a large factory owned by the Rockwell Corporation.

Phyllis became engaged to a fellow named Bob following high school, and then came to work as a private secretary in the purchasing department of Rockwell. About the same time I was promoted into Rockwell's engineering department where Phyllis often came to copy contracts. She was a beautiful young lady and immediately caught my eye.

One day after she left with her copies, the elderly fellow who operated the copying machine looked over at me and said, "Bill, you kinda' like her don't you?" I smiled and said, "Yes, but she has a ring on her finger, so there's nothing I can do." He looked at me and said something so profound that it stirred me into action and changed my life.

He said, "Bill, here's some advice. If you're thinking of making a move on her, I suggest you do it before she gets the second ring on her finger."

That thought had never crossed my mind. But I was aware that every time I saw her 'swish' through the office, it stirred my emotions. After thinking it over, I decided to ask her for a date. I was surprised and pleased when she agreed. Since she was engaged we agreed to ask one of her girlfriends to go along as a sort of chaperone.

Phyllis lived with her parents in a small neighborhood, and her girlfriend lived three houses away on the opposite side of the street. The day finally arrived for our chaperoned date. I drove to the girlfriend's house and went inside. The girls seemed nervous and I quickly noticed that Phyllis had removed her engagement ring.

Suddenly a loud angry voice came blasting in from the street. It was Phyllis' father and he was raging mad. Phyllis had told her parents she was going to a movie with her girlfriend, but she hadn't said they were going with anyone else. She had removed her ring and told them she was ending her engagement to Bob.

When Phyllis' father saw me drive by and go inside the house where the girls were, he went ballistic with rage. He used words that would shame most grown-ups and ordered Phyllis out of the house. The girls decided to walk to the movie theater about a mile away. They knew they had to get away quickly to appease his anger.

Both looked shocked and embarrassed as they left. I stood alone in the front room and remembered the touching look on Phyllis' face as she left. It seemed to say, "I'm so sorry Bill, but everything is in your hands now." I don't know how long I stood alone in the house before the shock began to wear off.

I was stunned that a father could talk that way to his daughter, especially to someone as wonderful as Phyllis. I couldn't believe all the things I had just heard from the mouth of a total stranger.

I was still reeling inside as I walked to my car and sat down with the door open. I remembered the suffering look on Phyllis' face as she listened to her father's voice, and I remembered the tender look in her eyes when she left. I sat in my car a long time and finally decided I had only two choices:

I could simply drive away, forget about Phyllis and never look back. Or I could follow my heart and ask her parents to talk with me.

I had never been faced with this kind of decision before. I was uneasy, but my feelings for Phyllis became so strong I decided to talk to her parents. Deep inside I knew this could be a defining moment in my life. I also knew in my heart that it was what I wanted to do. I had to win her parent's approval to make things right.

I put my car in reverse until it rolled to a stop in front of her parents' home. Then with great apprehension I slowly approached her parents who were sitting on their porch.

After introducing myself I said, "I'm sorry for any trouble I caused by asking Phyllis to go to the movie with me. Please let me tell you how I feel and how this all came about." Thank God it worked! Their mood softened and I received their approval to date Phyllis.

When Phyllis saw what I had done, how I faced her angry father instead of running away, she knew she had a winner. This was when our cleaving started.

After we had dated a short time, she invited me to her house in the evenings to watch TV which was something new in most homes. Since I lived alone in a small apartment this was a real treat for me and gave me the opportunity to spend time with Phyllis and her parents. Soon after, she invited me to attend Church and Sunday school with her.

This was something new that I had never done before. A life-changing encounter with God had occurred about a year before I met Phyllis. It happened one lonely night as I sat in my car reading a small red Gideon Bible, given to me during high school. It was such a profound spiritual experience that it turned me around and changed my life forever.

It didn't take long for both of us to know in our hearts that we were meant for each other. We began to plan the wedding and were married within the year. Our honeymoon was an eye opening trip by car to Niagara Falls, along Skyline Drive, and into Washington, D.C.

The photographs shown with the Introduction to this book were taken at our wedding and later with our first-born daughter when we lived in Kenton, Ohio.

We lived a short time in my small apartment before moving into a house near her parents. Ironically it was the same house where I met Phyllis and her friend for our first date. We continued working at Rockwell and about two years later Phyllis decided to leave her job and become a full time homemaker. Nine months later she became a full time mother.

My professional engineering career took us first to Columbus, Ohio and eventually to Port Orange, Florida. We were in love and happily married for nearly 44 years until her death. It was a wonderful marriage full of excitement, change, growth, and love.

We both became active in church activities. Phyllis became an adult Bible class teacher, while I attended seminary classes and was certified by the governing church body to conduct worship services, preach, teach, and manage church affairs.

As our family grew and our lives prospered we traveled the USA from New York to Hawaii and enjoyed the numerous blessings that God so graciously bestowed upon us.

CHAPTER SIX

HER TIME OUT

❖ ❖ ❖ ❖ ❖

NOW LET ME TELL YOU WHEN, WHY, AND HOW the initial perception of cleaving eventually crystallized in my mind. Phyllis and I had been married about 40 years. Our children were grown and we had settled into an empty-nest lifestyle in Florida.

It was just an ordinary day when, out of the blue, Phyllis came into the living room and said very calmly, "I'm leaving." I could see from her face that she was serious, so I didn't object.

I asked, "Where are you going?" and she said, "I don't know, and I don't know when I'll be back." Then she packed some clothes, got into our car and left. I was anxious, but I said goodbye and watched her drive away.

After she had gone I started to worry about her safety on the road alone. I knew the car was safe, but I was nervous about not knowing where she was going or when I would see her again. For the very first time in our lives we were both on our own, all alone, and I had no way to reach her or protect her.

I sat at the kitchen table and stared silently into space, as my mind filled with questions.

Was she mad or upset with me?

Did I do or say something to hurt her?

Was she seriously ill and didn't want me to know about it?

As these and many more questions ran through my mind, I began to think about and analyze our marriage. I had always been a faithful husband, father, and bread-winner and she had always been a faithful wife, mother, and homemaker. Our three children had turned out well and our love life had been fulfilling. Our marriage bond had always been secure, even during times of stress.

What was missing? What caused her to leave? Moreover, how was I going to handle this desertion? What choices did I have? As I asked these questions, I began to pray for understanding. That's when the scripture in Genesis 2:24 came to me, "Therefore shall a man leave his father and his mother, and shall cleave unto his wife: and they shall be one flesh."

I thought to myself, "What does God mean by the word cleave?" I went immediately to the dictionary. After reading words like, a cutting blow, penetrate, and adhere firmly, I began to see a familiar picture appear.

My mind drifted back to my experience as a boy splitting firewood, when my axe would stick in the tree round and I could not get it free. I slowly realized that this could be how a Godly marriage appears to God, "A man and his wife sticking together for life."

My spirits lifted because that was how God saw me cleaving to Phyllis. I could see that when we were apart, she was not alone, because I was still cleaved to her. I could not be moved away from her unless an outside wedge forced us apart. Even though her hasty trip puzzled me, I began to realize a couple of very important things about marriage:

1. If you love someone, set them free, and if they love you, they will return.
2. The wife is the underpinning of the marriage and the husband is cleaved to her.

This means that if she is unhappy, he is going to be unhappy; when her mood changes, the husband's mood changes. In other words, "A happy wife means a happy life."

After two nights of worrying and wondering if she was safe, Phyllis called to let me know she was fine, and was coming home the next day. I silently thanked God for her phone call.

She had driven south over 100 miles along the coastline before stopping at a resort we had previously visited together. She remained there in solitude for three days.

While waiting for her return it dawned on me that Phyllis had never spent any time alone before. She was living with her parents when we met, and moved into my apartment when we married. Unlike many young women who left their home to attend college, Phyllis had lived her entire life either in the company of her parents or me.

Our reunion was quiet and for some reason I felt good inside. She only told me that she suddenly felt the need to get away and reconnect with herself. She just wanted to see if she could accomplish something alone and hadn't meant to cause worry.

She thanked me for understanding and after sharing with her my insights about cleaving, I prayed again silently, "Thank you, God."

Unnoticed at the time were the small, but subtle, changes that occurred after her time alone. She began to relax more and to seize greater pleasure in the activities we shared together as her reserved demeanor gave way to boldness and excitement.

A few years later, Phyllis died suddenly from a silent heart defect. By the time she passed away, our lives had been blessed with three wonderful children and six grandchildren.

My personal grief and loneliness would have been overwhelming without God's help and the love and support of my family and friends.

CHAPTER SEVEN

TWO BECOME ONE

❖ ❖ ❖ ❖ ❖

LET'S TAKE A DEEPER LOOK AT THIS UNIQUE alliance called marriage. Ideally, the marriage celebration takes place after the man is cleaved to his wife. It is a public ceremony and legally sets the couple apart in the community and the world.

Displays of affection and intimate sexual endeavors that were forbidden before are now sanctioned by God. There is no humiliation or shame associated with their intimacies and sexual acts of love. They are free to fulfill their fantasies and to privately enjoy the wonderful joys of being a man and wife cleaved together.

Although God blesses and guards marriage partners He also knows that life will test their commitments. He knows evil can infiltrate a marriage through normal everyday activities; that it is lurking where you least expect it; and that it has few limits and may come in many disguises.

We can be thankful that God promised to protect and defend our marriage commitments against the evil that lurks everywhere.

God knows that when the husband has not completely cleaved unto his wife the basic marriage structure is on shaky ground. When He is forced to work with the wife and husband as two individuals, instead of one, the marriage loses much of its spiritual power.

Happy and blessed is the marriage where the husband and wife are cleaved together from the beginning.

Why Do Marriages Succeed

Time after time it is the courting experience that leads to lifelong connections and bonding. It is the time when passion rules the heart and commitments are made with each other.

As the mountaineer lady said to a young minister during his first interview for the job of church pastor, "If you ain't heard nothin' and you ain't seen nothin' and you ain't felt nothin' then you probably ain't got nothin'."

That is what cleaving is all about. It takes passion to bring a man's heart into the receptive soul of his wife, and it takes total commitment to keep it in place. It is a time when the simple act of hand-holding sends the heart leaping and emotions soaring. It is a time when the heart and the head work together as one.

Based upon God's original intent, marriage is a special place where our personal issues can be purified and we can return to a state of wholeness. Marriage is a sanctified relationship that demands constant attention by the man to the needs of his wife in order to survive and to thrive. It requires unconditional love, respect, faithfulness and tenderness.

Total commitment to each other! I am convinced that marriages succeed because the husband and the wife know in their souls that only death itself can separate them. When bad times happen, the spiritual bond of cleaving kicks in to save them and hold them together.

Our culture thrusts huge temptations upon all couples during marriage. As a result about half of the couples in our society lose their way and head for divorce courts

Many of the problems within marriage show up in the form of sexual temptations. We should recognize that both partners may be tempted at some point. Based on the nature of man, this is especially true for the husband. Unless the couple is very diligent in keeping their sexual relationship vibrant, his eyes will start to wander and his thoughts stray.

How does cleaving help?

It kicks in by slowly refocusing his thoughts back to his wife and family. It reminds him of his marriage commitment first and then of his need for intervention in order to overcome the temptation. No man has the will power to resist until he asks God for divine intervention.

I recall from my own experiences that the mental awareness of needing help during a sexual temptation would then lead me into prayer. I would pray that the temptation be divinely removed from my presence which then enabled me to thank God for removing it. God never placed me under condemnation when these instances occurred, always under grace.

Why Do Marriages Run Into Trouble

A basic understanding of what God meant by cleaving helps us shed some light on most marriage problems. I am convinced that without the cleaving encounter with its holding power, all marriages are on a slippery slope.

Without the many benefits of the cleaving experience, basic human passions can and do take over. Without cleaving that special spark that was present during courtship can diminish and go out. Without cleaving the divine nature of marriage is missing and divorce can rear its ugly head and destroy the marriage.

I do not in any way consider myself an authority on divorce. However, I have observed with interest the divorce proceedings of several family members and friends during the past several decades. They had legitimate reasons for separating. However, when their actions are examined through the lenses of cleaving, their marriages seemed to falter because the deep bond of cleaving was missing. When the going got tough, God's powerful act of cleaving was not called upon to pull them through.

Consider now these questions. When the going gets tough, what will you rely on to save your marriage? If you rely only on feelings and memories and good intentions, can you stick it out?

Based on my personal experiences covering over 50 years of marriage, I don't believe so. As I recall, whenever a severe crisis came into my marriage, I always relied on my cleaving bond and prayer to pull me through.

CHAPTER EIGHT

TEARING THEM APART

❖ ❖ ❖ ❖ ❖

DEATH OR DIVORCE ... EITHER WAY MARRIAGE separations are extremely traumatic?

Returning to our image of the axe cleaved into the tree round, we saw that the bond could only be separated by driving a steel wedge through the tree round.

In a marriage, separation can take the form of either death or divorce. Let us look first at the biological separation caused by death, and then at the mandatory severance brought about by divorce.

In a Godly marriage only the natural death of a spouse should separate the couple. When death occurs, the marriage covenant ends and the surviving spouse is free to move on with his or her life. Since death is final, it brings closure quickly. That is why God will always intervene to protect and help the survivor through the grieving process.

Civil divorce is a different situation because the marriage is wedged apart in the courts through legal actions and proceedings. This requires unambiguous actions by at least one of the parties in order to break the marriage contract. The husband, like the axe, often separates from the marriage with little emotional damage. But the wife, like the round, always suffers poignant scars, especially if the husband was non-caring or intentionally hurtful.

Tearing a marriage apart through divorce is more brutal than tearing it apart by death. Returning to our image of the axe in the tree round, we see that damage always occurs as the wedge forces the wood to separate. It always leaves a scar where the bond held them together. Because of the tearing, divorce is not something God had in mind at the beginning.

Jesus confirmed this in Matthew 19:7-8 while speaking to the Pharisees; "They (the Pharisees) say unto him, Why did Moses then command to give a writing of divorcement, and to put her away? He (Jesus) saith unto them, Moses because of the hardness of your hearts suffered you to put away your wives: but from the beginning it was not so."

Many will argue that divorce is the only solution to an abusive marriage and God agrees. Abuses can manifest within the marriage in many forms and usually stems from the three basic human weaknesses of lust, greed, and pride that Jesus overcame in the wilderness by the word of God.

What do you think would happen if the type of cleaving described in this book occurred before the marriage? Would it prevent divorce from happening? Would it prevent the fears and scaring of the children? You bet it would.

The scriptures teach us that God never intended for the marriage union to be torn apart by divorce when He instructed man to cleave unto his wife. Cleaving is so powerful that it doesn't allow any wiggle room for divorce to enter. Cleaving truly wraps the whole family in spiritual armor.

Just as the sharp edge of the cleaved axe is buried deep inside the wood, so are the eyes of the married man buried deep within his wife and his family. When temptations appear the husband's sexual interest and feelings may be aroused but the power of cleaving will always redirect his focus to his wife and family and prayer will see him through to safety.

To visualize a marriage that is unstable, we can picture a woodsman who uses little effort when he swings his axe into the tree round. Consequently, the blade hardly sticks to the wood. With little sticking power between the axe and the round, each can be easily moved.

Sadly, this is the shallow image of a man and woman who are only partially committed to their marriage. The marriage bond that God sustains through cleaving is missing. There is little sticking power between the couple and they can easily be drawn away from each other by lust or distractions.

The fact that cleaving is ordained by God means that it will overcome all obstacles in its path. In a Godly marriage, spiritual cleaving occurs before the wedding takes place. In fact, the evidence of cleaving often becomes apparent during the wedding ceremony. This is a time of high stress and anxiety as the final vows are pledged between the couple.

By observing the wedding panorama, the level of commitment is revealed as the bride and groom interact with each other. You can easily spot a couple with a cleaving attitude because they are always trying to please and help each other. On the other hand, you can spot the lack of commitment when the bride and groom seem absorbed in their own worlds and fail to see, and even ignore, their mate's needs or desires.

Whenever I have observed only a moderate commitment at a wedding, the marriage union would eventually head in the direction of divorce. Perhaps when we properly understand God's motive for cleaving, we can reverse the high divorce figures in this country. What a wonderful improvement that would be for us.

Recently teams of experts, made up of attorneys, financial specialists, and therapists, have collaborated to guide couples through the divorce process. Wouldn't it be great if there were a safe way to inform men and women of the hazards they may encounter during the dating and courting process.

Reading this book before dating would uniquely prepare them for courtship later. With a knowledgeable understanding of Genesis 2:24, they could properly evaluate their choices and the depth of their emotional commitments. Only then would they move toward marriage.

CHAPTER NINE

HEALING TIME

❖ ❖ ❖ ❖ ❖

BOTH DEATH AND DIVORCE REQUIRE HEALING through an emotional process called grief. Grief is powerful and will take its own path through the mind, the body, and the spirit. I have experienced the death of my wife and closely observed the damage inflicted on others by divorce. An interesting thing I have observed is that healing seems to take less time and be less painful following a death than it does after a divorce.

Is there an explanation?

First, let us look at grief that follows the death of a spouse. Since death means the end of a life it is a traumatic experience for the one left behind. However, it is a natural event and the grieving cycle seems to follow a definite path to its conclusion. Death is actually a part of living and should be accepted as neither good nor bad. It just is! The best way to honor the end of life is by comforting families as they go through the pain of losing their loved one.

Sometimes death is sudden and sometimes it follows a long illness. I have observed two patterns in the grieving process suffered by survivors. Sudden death increases the intensity of the grief but usually ends in a relatively short period of time. Long term care-giving for a loved one may bring a lower level of grieving but takes place over a longer period of time. It appears the overall amount of pain is about the same in both situations.

The death of my wife was very sudden and traumatic. She died in our car as we traveled to meet with friends in another state. We were cruising along an Interstate Highway, in the middle of the night listening to the radio, when her heart failed. She had a medical condition called cardiac arrhythmia. For some unknown reason her medication failed to protect her and she passed away during the brief time it took for me to safely pull off the highway and stop. There was nothing I could do to help her.

Needless to day, her instantaneous death caused me intense heart-throbbing pain and anguish. My only consolation was that she appeared to quietly fall asleep without any sign of pain. God immediately intervened on my behalf and sent a wonderful Christian pastor and his wife to walk me safely through my trauma and the initial grieving process.

Divorce, on the other hand, takes a different path and the grief that follows may be slow in coming. Therefore, the healing process is going to be different and may last several years. Unlike death, there is no final closure in divorce. It is a legal dissolution of a marriage.

The grief that follows divorce can be very serious. It may be expressed by a combination of hostile anger and deep depression that can last a long time. The support of a trusted friend is always essential in working through this grief successfully.

At some point the grief that follows death and divorce should end. It is important to avoid getting stuck in the middle of the grieving process. You must continuously look forward and move forward with your life. Grieving will only end by persistently moving through it.

Surviving these periods of grief, I believe, requires God's direct intervention. He is the master healer through His Son, Jesus the Christ. The Christ brings a grieving soul into the truths of God. The truth sets us free to live again and to claim our own true nature that is spiritual and perfect.

CHAPTER TEN

ULTIMATE CLEAVING

❖ ❖ ❖ ❖ ❖

HAVE YOU EVER WONDERED WHY JESUS IS called the bridegroom and the church is called His bride? Could it be that God is simply following His original creative strategy? Perhaps a spiritual understanding of cleaving will enlighten us about God's plan of redemption.

Follow along as God implements His plan to save mankind.

Like a woodsman swinging his axe solidly into a tree round, God initiated His divine plan by sending Jesus the Christ into the world and cleaving Him unto his bride, the church. Jesus understood His divine mission and accepted the role of bridegroom. Then He proved God's ultimate love by giving His life to establish the church as his true bride.

The role of Jesus is described brilliantly in the first verse of one of my favorite hymns. "The church's one foundation is Jesus Christ her Lord; she is His new creation by water and the word; from heaven He came and sought her to be His holy bride; with His own blood He bought her, and for her life He died."

We know Satan is always trying to drive a wedge into the church and tear Jesus away. He employs the basic human weaknesses of lust, greed, and pride in his attempt to separate Jesus from the church. Satan knows that cleaving does not allow any wiggle room for his deceptions. His evil power is always defeated by applying God's word to the temptation facing us. In the wilderness Jesus rebuked Satan three times using the word of God as revealed in Matthew 4:1-11.

Jesus proved by His death and resurrection that He will never leave His bride. I am reminded of Jesus' commitment every time I see a picture of Him nailed to the cross. A friend described the scene this way. While He was hanging on the cross, He looked ahead in time, and as He was dying on the cross we were on His mind, and He said, "Father, forgive them; for they know not what they do." (Luke 23:34).

God listened and granted His Son's request. The church and all mankind were forgiven. In fulfilling His role, Jesus proved beyond any doubt that He loved His bride. Jesus showed by that example what it truly means for a man to love his wife and never leave her.

When we understand God's divine plan to redeem His church, we gain insight into the many marriage problems in our society. Most divorces take place because the husband has not become totally committed to loving his wife.

It is the husband's duty to know the depth of his personal commitment to his bride before the wedding takes place.

When we understand that cleaving means total commitment in God's eyes, we can see God's strategy more clearly. He presented a magnificent divine vision for mankind when in

Genesis 2:24, He said, "Therefore shall a man leave his father and mother, and shall cleave unto his wife: and they shall be one flesh."

The image of Jesus cleaving unto the church is an exact model of a Godly marriage. Lest we might think cleaving is confined to an Old Testament concept, we only need to look at how Jesus applied the same response to a question about divorce, when He was tempted by the Pharisees.

In Matthew 19: 3-6 we read, "The Pharisees also came unto him, tempting him, and saying unto him, Is it lawful for a man to put away his wife for every cause? And he answered and said unto them, Have ye not read, that he which made them at the beginning made them male and female, And said, For this cause shall a man leave father and mother, and shall cleave to his wife: and they twain shall be one flesh? Wherefore they are no more twain, but one flesh. What therefore God hath joined together, let not man put asunder."

The Scriptures clearly state that a Godly marriage includes the cleaving of both the husband and the wife. Jesus made it very clear that God never intended for any man to divorce his wife when he added, "What therefore God hath joined together, let not man put asunder." God gave man many choices, but leaving his wife is not one of them.

In Genesis we can clearly see that God's ultimate plan for mankind began by cleaving a man to his wife and ended by cleaving Jesus to the church. If we do not want to accept God's definition of marriage, what can we do? Since marriage really is all about cleaving, what options do we have?

We can deny that God exists. We can deny that Jesus is the Christ. We can deny that marriage was instituted and blessed by God. But we cannot deny, however, that marriage requires total commitment to hold it together.

When cleaving does not take place in the marriage, there seems to be little hope for the relationship to survive. We need look no further than Jesus and the church to see how seriously God envisioned marriage between a man and his wife.

CHAPTER ELEVEN

CLEAVING IS NOT LEAVING

❖ ❖ ❖ ❖ ❖

THROUGHOUT THIS BOOK WE HAVE LOOKED AT cleaving in a variety of situations. First we looked at natural cleaving when the tree round seized the axe. We then witnessed emotional cleaving when a husband deeply loved his wife. Additionally we saw divine cleaving when Jesus willingly died for His bride, the church.

Cleaving is a decision to totally commit your self to your marriage. The greatest significance of cleaving is that it is an open ended obligation and applies to everything you do. The truth is that it doesn't take much of a man to make this decision, but it does take all there is of him to fulfill it. Like pregnancy, marriage is a total obligation for those who make the commitment.

It is a decision that you make one time which sets your course during the remainder of your marriage. How then do you know if you have become totally committed to your marriage?

There is a "three question rule" you can use to guide your thoughts and keep you on track. This rule can be used in any of life's situations, but it works especially well in your marriage. These are the questions:

1. Is what I'm doing best for my spouse?
2. Is what I'm doing best for our marriage?
3. Is what I'm doing best for me?

The rule states that you must say "yes" to all three questions, in the same order, if you want to proceed with what you are doing. Two out of three will not work, so don't go there. If you cannot answer "yes" to all three, then stop.

My first objective in writing this book is to stimulate your mind with the idea that God meant what He said about cleaving and that He said what He meant. My second is to show you that "cleaving is not leaving."

After He cleaved man unto his wife, God issued His very first commandment in Genesis 1:28. He told them to become sexually active when He said, "Be fruitful and multiply."

I believe God intentionally placed personal commitment before sexual activity. He knew that life was going to be sexually transmitted and wanted to make it one of mankind's greatest pleasures. One night sexual hook-ups, and prostitution of the body for money, are not part of God's plan.

When we condone or participate in sex without commitment, we start down a road of misery and self destruction.

This book does not deal with the myriad problems that can occur during marriage. I did not include them because they only divert attention away from the book's purpose of demonstrating that marriage really is all about cleaving.

I was pleased to see that God saw no inherent problems when He developed His strategy for marriage, sex, and life. In fact, Genesis 1:31 records that He looked upon all that He had made in six days and, "it was very good."

Cleaving is very good. Marriage is very good. Sex is very good. Life is very good. God takes them seriously, and so should we by following His principles and guidelines in our daily lives.

Various thoughts on cleaving have been discussed within these pages to give you insight on marriage and to enrich your understanding of how well a marriage can function when it is based upon Holy Scripture.

God reveals through cleaving, that we are not human beings going through a temporary marriage experience; in Genesis we see that we are really married people going through a temporary human experience.

Before closing the book, let me share with you the following words of advice for keeping the flame of passion alive in your marriage:

Regardless of your age always remember the very first 'touch with intent' that you shared with your loved one. That electric moment that sent your heart leaping. That simple act of 'hand-holding' that sent your emotions flooding when you first met the person you married.

Remember too that magical moment of commitment when he anxiously said, 'Will you marry me?' and the soft breathtaking answer … 'Yes, I will.' It is the gentle touch of loving hands at unexpected times that will tug at your hearts and bring unbelievable happiness to both of you.

We only regard those unions as real examples of love and real marriages in which a fixed and unalterable decision has been taken. If men or women contemplate an escape, they do not collect all their powers for the task. In none of the serious and important tasks of life do we arrange such a "getaway." We cannot love and be limited.　　　　　　　—Alfred Adler

SCRIPTURE REFERENCES

❖ ❖ ❖ ❖ ❖

All scriptures quotations are taken from the Author-ized King James Version (KJV) 1611.

http://www.jesus-is-lord.com/thebible.htm

Introduction___ Genesis 2:24

Life is Sexually
Transmitted __ Genesis 2:24
Ecclesiastes 12:13
Genesis 1:27-28

A Picture of
Cleaving __ I Corinthians 11:3

Choices Mold
Our Lives___ Genesis 1:3-4 & 31
Ephesians 5:22, 25, 28 & 6:1-4

God's Hidden
Secrets __Genesis 2:24
Matthew 14:27-31
Romans 8:14
Revelations 12:10
James1:5 & 4:17

The Turning Point __Romans 14:8

Her Time Out __Genesis 2:24

Tearing Them
Apart __Matthew 19:7-8

The Ultimate
Cleaving __Matthew 4:1-11 & 19:3-6
Luke 23:34
Genesis 2:24

Cleaving Is
Not Leaving __Genesis 1:28 & 31

The Grand essentials of happiness are: something to do, something to love, and something to hope for.
—Allan K. Chalmers

God meant what He said in Genesis 2:24 and society pays a heavy price when it is not under-stood or cast aside.
—William A. Cummins

EVERY LOVE STORY IN THIS BOOK IS A STORY OF CLEAVING

❖ ❖ ❖ ❖ ❖

HAVE YOU EVER HAD THE URGE TO WRITE down your love story for your children? I asked this question and several friends responded. Each story is a true story written in their own words.

The evidence of cleaving is manifested in their total commitment to marriage, which led them to sexual fulfillment, and happiness.

They are included in my book to show you how important courtship is in God's plan. I believe you will enjoy reading every one of these stories of love and that they will affect your life in a positive way.

If I am not worth the wooing, I am surely
not worth the winning.
> —Henry Wadsworth Longfellow

I am like a falling star who has finally found her
place next to another in a lovely constellation,
where we will sparkle in the heavens forever.
> —Amy Tan

PART TWO CONTENTS

❖   ❖   ❖   ❖   ❖

Love seems the swiftest, but it is the slowest of all growths. No man or woman really knows what perfect love is until they have been married a quarter of a century.   —Mark Twain

1
A SMILE, PASSION, AND TWO WILLING HEARTS

"Cleaving as if by Destiny"
Bill and Ann

❖　❖　❖　❖　❖

IT WAS THANKSGIVING. BILL HAD TRAVELED 900 miles to visit his children and grandchildren and to attend a business conference. Charlie and Rosie had just joined his business team and thought their friend, Ann, might be interested in the business too. Rosie had graduated high school with Ann and said she would call her to make the arrangements.

Rosie knew that Ann had been divorced several years earlier, after about 30 years of marriage. She knew Ann had a comfortable home and had worked hard to make it her own. Rosie also knew that Bill's wife had died very suddenly after almost 44 years of marriage and that he would only be in Ohio a few more days before returning to Florida.

Ann was busy at work when Rosie called and told her what Bill was doing in town, Ann said, "I remember Bill. We graduated from the same high school. He was a few years ahead of me and lived on the farm next to my parents when we were still in school."

Ann reminisced that Bill always had a smile on his face. She could still see him getting on a school bus when she was about ten years old and remembered as he turned to say something, he smiled. She had always remembered that smile but had no idea what Bill was doing and never really thought about him after high school.

Rosie explained that Bill would be calling her, but Ann was reluctant to talk to anyone. Rosie encouraged Ann by saying, "Ann, he's a gorgeous man and I want you to talk to him." So Ann agreed to wait for Bill's call the next day.

When he didn't call, Ann was adamant and said to Rosie, "During the last nine years I've

met enough jerks, so just forget this one too."
Rosie immediately called Bill and said, "You'd
better call Ann because I promised her you
would. She's one of my best friends and besides that; she is a really gorgeous lady."

Ann was very surprised when Bill called her
at work on the Friday after Thanksgiving. After
some small talk, they agreed to meet on Sunday
after church at a small local restaurant. Ann
wasn't especially interested in Bill's business
and figured she might want to get away fast, so
she drove her car for a quick escape. How little they knew about what was coming.

When Bill's eyes met Ann's at the restaurant,
he immediately felt a warming inside. He wasn't
alone in these feelings. When Ann's eyes saw the
smile on Bill's face some old memories flood-
ed back. They greeted each other with a small
hug and big smiles.

The restaurant was busy when they arrived,
so Ann suggested they go to another restaurant
a few blocks away. As they walked toward Bill's
car, he reached down and squeezed Ann's
hand. She said nothing as Bill helped her into
his car. After Bill seated himself, he leaned over

and lightly kissed Ann's cheek. He could feel something stirring in his emotions. Ann smiled but did not resist. Nothing was said.

The waitress must have seen their need for seclusion and seated them in a quiet corner. They ordered food that they didn't eat, and drank lots of iced tea. Their meeting soon turned into hours of intimate conversations about the past, families, kids, school pals, and dreams. By evening the sensual stirrings were stronger and Ann's perfume filled the air. Things heated up and Ann did something she had never done before. She said, "Bill would you like to come to my home where we can talk some more?" Without hesitation he agreed. Ann and her sweet perfume had taken hold of his emotions.

At Ann's home their talking soon turned into touching hands, hugs, and kisses. Time was standing still for Bill and Ann and they didn't want it to end. They seemed to become physically and emotionally entwined as they enjoyed their precious time together. Something exciting had come into their lives. Bill didn't want to leave, but since he was returning to Florida the next day he had to go. After a final long, passionate kiss he left.

As he drove away he tried to analyze what was happening, but couldn't. All he could do was smile. He knew his life was changing. Ann felt the same. What had happened to them? Would she see him again? Would he call? She was drained emotionally and physically but happy inside, so she smiled sadly as she watched him drive out of sight.

The next day Bill headed home, or so he thought. His Cadillac pulled onto the interstate and turned not toward Florida, but toward the city where Ann lived and worked. An hour later he found himself in her office building talking to the receptionist.

When Ann got the call from the receptionist, she shrieked, "What's he doing here?" All her co-workers heard her yell and asked what was happening. Ann briefly explained what had happened on Sunday, and while Ann was meeting with Bill, they all streamed by the reception area to take a peek at her suitor.

Bill was aglow when he saw Ann and gave her a kiss and a hug. He said, "I just had to see you again before I left. I can't get you out of my mind." Ann mumbled something about how surprised she was and said, "I've been thinking of you too." Bill asked Ann if she had ever been to Florida. Ann said, "I don't like the Miami area, too many bugs." He asked her if she would consider visiting his home near Daytona Beach to see where he lived, and assured her it was different from the Miami area.

Something sensual was happening to both of them. Bill drove the 900 miles without stopping except for gas and to call Ann. He rested the next day but called Ann during her morning and afternoon office breaks. They also talked for hours each night. Their attraction to each other grew stronger and stronger each time they chatted.

By midweek Bill was ready to make his move. He asked Ann to fly down for the week end and assured her that, "You'll be back in time for work on Monday." He said that all arrangements had been made for her trip. All she had to do was park her car at the airport, pick up her tickets, and get on the plane. Ann said softly, "OK, I'll do it."

After agreeing to visit Bill, Ann made the necessary arrangements and on Friday evening drove to the airport. She locked her car, one of her most valued possessions, and picked up the ticket waiting for her. As her plane left the runway several thoughts started running through her mind, "What am I doing? Bill and I met only five days ago and here I am on my way to spend the weekend with him in Florida. Why did I agree to do this?" But a strange, warm excitement was tugging at her heart. She smiled and closed her eyes as the plane swiftly moved her through the night sky.

During the week, Bill's emotions became highly aroused whenever he thought of Ann. He couldn't stop his excitement over seeing her again. He decided to purchase the perfume she used that always stirred his passion when she was near. Very quickly, hundreds of dollars worth of her favorite perfume arrived at his home. Every day he thought of a new surprise for her. By Friday he had everything arranged and was ready for her visit.

It was late Friday night when Ann arrived in Orlando. Bill played love songs for her on the way home in his car. She felt warm as they held hands and drove silently through the night. After parking in the driveway, Bill said, "Close your eyes" and they walked to the front door.

Upon entering he said, "Open your eyes" and she saw a beautiful living room. Waiting for her on a small draped table was champagne, a gold watch, and a red rose in a bud vase. She could hear romantic music softly playing in the background.

Ann could feel herself tingle inside as she searched the scene. Bill said, "Close your eyes again," as he led her gently through a long hall-way and into another large room. She held her breath with anticipation as she wondered where she was going and what was happening.

The room was bathed in soft light as she opened her eyes. She gazed at a beautiful bed draped in soft white linen. The center of the bed was piled high with her favorite perfume on a beautiful purple velvet box. The arrangement of gift boxes also draped in soft linen made for a spectacular display and one happy lady.

Bill stood behind her as her senses soared. Then she saw the small card with a ribbon hold-ing Bill's wedding band. She knew he had not taken it off since his beloved wife had died. She could feel her senses reeling as she picked up the card and the ring. She began to feel faint.

When she opened the card, she saw a small blue ribbon across the bottom of the card. With trembling fingers she slowly lifted the ribbon and saw the hidden words, "Ann, Will You Marry Me?" Her body shook as her legs lost their strength and Bill caught her in his gentle arms.

Shaken by it all, she slowly turned in his arms, and with a beautiful smile on her face and through trembling lips she said, "Yes." For several minutes he held her in his arms. They kissed lovingly and long while the passion of the evening held them in its grasp.

They spent most of the night talking about their new lives together and about the huge changes coming into their lives, but they mostly bathed in the bloom of the fantastic new love bond that had made them feel alive again. A whole new life was waiting for them and it felt GOOD.

Bill prepared breakfast the next morning and the conversation continued on for most of the day. There was still much to talk about. In the evening Bill and Ann dined at a restaurant that overlooked a beautiful river. The restaurant became one of their favorites and Danish Lobster Tails became their favorite meal.

Ann had plans to go to California to spend the Christmas holiday with her oldest son and his family. Bill wanted to make sure she had a ring on her finger before she left, so he made another nonstop road trip to Ohio in awful winter weather. Then a short trip with Ann to a nearby mall produced an engagement ring for her.

When Ann had returned from California, Bill picked her up on his way to Nashville to attend a business conference. Several of his close business associates made it known they were thrilled that Bill had found someone. One man, Willie, ran across the auditorium and whisked Ann off her feet thanking her for putting a smile on Bill's face. He said Bill had been like a lost puppy and his friends were worried about him.

In February, Bill and Ann flew to Las Vegas to be married in the 'Little White Chapel' on the famous Vegas Strip. It was a beautiful wedding with a pastor, organist, and limousine service to and from the cozy wedding chapel. Their close friends, Rosie and Charlie, were matron-of-honor and best-man. Ann's son, Scott, gave her away under the watchful eye of his family and Bill's older brother, Jack.

After the wedding, Bill and Ann had a lovely dinner with everyone in the wedding party, and then spent the rest of the week in Las Vegas.

Later on, in May, Bill and Ann flew to Hawaii for two weeks on the island of Maui. They had a relaxing time and plan to visit it again some day. Returning home to Florida was wonderful too, as their new lives unfolded before them.

All it took was his smile, her sweet perfume, and two willing hearts.

2
CLIMBING THE CONVENT WALLS

"Cleaving Despite Circumstances"
Carol and Doc

❖ ❖ ❖ ❖ ❖

CAROL AND TWO OF HER SISTERS HAD entered the Catholic Convent, and Carol had spent the last 12 years as a nun. Carol was introduced to a local doctor at a community dance. Doc had already separated from his wife because of an unhappy marriage. With urging from their friends, Carol and Doc agreed to dance together. At the end of the dance Carol said, "Doctor, the music has stopped, we can go sit down now" to which he answered, "No sister, the music hasn't stopped. Guess what sister; I'm going to marry you."

As she turned to join the other nuns, Carol chuckled and said, "Right, go have another drink with your cronnies." Doc said, "Yes sister, I am going to marry you but there are two things I have to work out" to which Carol inquired, "And what might they be?" Doc answered with, "I have to get a divorce, and get you out of the convent."

From there the chase was on. Doc became totally committed to winning Carol's heart and hand, and Carol discovered that her heart was receptive. Doc called on some people in the parish and asked them to help him contact Carol inside the convent. Then Doc pursued Carol, with poetry notes, little gifts, and a special poem with an 'angel's feather' taped onto it. No phone calls were made because Doc knew he was treading on sacred territory.

Finally, Carol decided to leave the convent and busy herself with a new life that allowed companionship with real people. She had done all that was possible within the convent and knew she must move on to fulfill God's plan for her life. She met with Mother Superior, her teacher during her first three grades of catholic school. Mother Superior was very kind and quite perceptive. Her first words were, "I knew you would leave someday; I just didn't know when." That made it much easier for Carol.

Mother Superior sent the paperwork for Carol's dispensation to the Holy Father in Rome. The dispensation was returned within two weeks and Carol left the convent community with $500. She located an apartment and began teaching at the Atterbury Job Corporation. The following weeks and months were filled with good moments and uneasy ones.

Doc applied for his divorce but he didn't get it as quickly as Carol got her dispensation. Although Doc's lawyer worked very hard, it still took five months to finalize his divorce. Divorce or no divorce, Doc was going to take Carol and her sister on a western tour of the United States in August before school began. The divorce became final just in time for them to leave for the fourteen-day tour.

During the ensuing months, arrangements were made for the so-called, "surprise wedding." During their courtship, Carol had showed Doc a lovely cemetery in nearby Brown County, which he later chose as the site for their wedding. Doc also ordered a special wedding bouquet for Carol. Among the dozen red rosebuds was one white rosebud that represented "forever."

Doc carried Carol across the threshold of his apartment and from then on he was always a soft place for her to fall. They were married for 26 years before Doc passed away. To this day, Carol continues to look for a companion who will continue to love her as her husband did.

Carol lovingly remembers Doc as someone who loved life. He was a medicine man, fisherman, hunter, and county commissioner. But most of all, he was her secret admirer.

3
SHORT, SWEET,
AND WONDERFUL

"Cleaving Immediately"
Roberta and Larry

❖ ❖ ❖ ❖ ❖

MY NAME IS ROBERTA. I MET LARRY THROUGH his twin brother and sister-in-law Barbara, whom I had known and grownup with from the age of eight. Larry and I were both 29 years old, had been married before, and I had two young sons. Larry was in the United States Air Force and was returning from a tour in Hawaii before transferring to Whiteman Air Force Base in Missouri.

My friend, Barbara, set us up on a blind date. On the day before the date, I really tried to back out simply because I had never been on a blind date before. It wasn't quite so blind on my part because by knowing Larry's twin brother, I had a pretty good idea about Larry's appearance. On October 21, 1971, I went with Larry to a pizza place in Columbus, Ohio. We had a wonderful time and saw each other only once more before he left for a temporary duty assignment. While he was gone we wrote and talked every day.

He told me that he knew when he saw me the first time, that I was the one for him. It was, "love at first sight" for him. I felt the same way. We learned a lot about each other in those daily letters and phone calls, and when he arrived back in Ohio, he produced an engagement ring and asked me to marry him!

We were married on November 26, 1971, in his brother's home by a pastor I had known since childhood.

After a brief honeymoon, he took me and my sons to his new home at Whiteman AFB, MO. If calculated, the time of our courtship was just 35 days and most of those days we were apart. We have now been married for over 34 wonderful years and that same spark still burns in our eyes and hearts.

I know God sent Larry into my life at just the right time to heal the hurt from my previous marriage. On the first day we met, and each day since, I have thanked God for sending Larry to me. We are wonderful friends and lovers. Larry accepted my sons as his own and God has blessed us with a beautiful daughter.

This is our love story, short, sweet, and wonderful.

4
LOVE AT FIRST SIGHT DOES EXIST

"Cleaving by the Sea"
Danielle and Chuck

❖ ❖ ❖ ❖ ❖

A VERY HIGH-SPIRITED GIRL NAMED DANIELLE lived in DeLand, Florida with her mom. Danielle's twin sister, Amber, lived in Daytona Beach with their dad but she spent weekends at the beach with her sister. One sunny weekend, Danielle and Amber went to the beach to meet up with Amber's boyfriend to play volleyball.

Danielle was sitting in the white sand when she glanced toward the water and saw a young man walking out of the ocean surf with a surfboard in hand. As she watched him walk toward her, a feeling of excitement, desire, and happiness rushed over her and she wondered if she would ever get a chance to meet him.

To her surprise, he walked up to her sister Amber and started talking. They attended school together and while they stood talking, Danielle was introduced to Chuck. When Danielle returned to her father's house, she told her step-mom that she had just met the man she was going to marry.

When Danielle returned home, she dreamed about Chuck almost every night. About a month later she was invited to another weekend party in Daytona. As she walked through house and into the kitchen, she suddenly saw Chuck. She became light headed, and when he remembered her name, she was enthralled.

She paid no attention to anyone else at the party. Danielle and Chuck talked the entire time about whatever came to mind. When the party ended her dream time with Chuck was over but her admiration for him had grown. It wasn't until after she had left the party that she realized she didn't have his phone number.

After weeks of feeling sorry for herself, Danielle was invited again to Daytona for a visit with one of her girlfriends. When she arrived at her friend's place, she was amazed to find that Chuck was living at the same residence. She spent all night visiting with the man in her dreams. Minute by minute Chuck was becoming even more than her dreams could imagine. Danielle finally got the courage to tell him she had a crush on him, and had felt that way since the day they first met. She got his phone number.

Danielle and Chuck talked almost every day and finally Chuck asked her out on their first date. He picked her up from home and met her family. They had a fabulous time. He took her to a haunted house in an amusement park and she held on to him the entire time.

Danielle decided to live with her father in Daytona, so she could be closer to her dream man. She finished high school and moved in with Chuck. After five exciting years of courtship she wanted her dream to become reality. She got down on her knees and proposed to him.

When Chuck declined her offer, her heart sank for a moment. Then he said that he was the one who should propose. When he did, she had a very quick answer. "Yes" she yelled.

The wedding was beautiful.

They were married near the river, with friends and family on hand to see her dream come true. When it was time to kiss the bride, he swept her off her feet and kissed her in a magical way. The man she had dreamed about, the man she loved so dearly, had now become her mate for life. Eight years and three children later, Danielle is still married to the man of her dreams.

5

WELL, YOU SURE DID GROW UP

"Cleaving in Military Time"
Lee and Dan

❖ ❖ ❖ ❖ ❖

MY NAME IS LEE. IT WAS A MONDAY IN AUGUST 1955, and the first day of my vacation from work. My mother and I were cleaning and painting my bedroom. We had taken a break to eat lunch when we saw a car drive up to the neighbor's house across the street. A sailor got out and walked to the front door. We were sure it was one of their grandsons, but we also knew that our neighbors were visiting their daughter in Pueblo. My mother insisted I go and tell him where they were, but I refused since I was in old dirty clothes and looked a mess.

My mother walked over to tell him. He listened and gave her a big hug before getting in his car and driving away. When mother told me the grandson's name was Dan, I wasn't impressed. I had known Dan as a kid and also in high school and remembered that he was very short and skinny. He was not exactly a young teenager's dream. He had graduated from high school two years before I did and joined the Navy. It had been four years since I'd last seen him.

That evening his cousin came to our home for dinner and I told him that Dan was home on leave. He wanted to see Dan so he called Dan's mother and made arrangements to go to her house. Not knowing exactly where she lived, he asked me to go along and help him find her home. I put on some makeup, pulled my hair into a ponytail and away we went. Dan came to the door and when he saw me he said, "Well, you sure did grow up!" One look at him and all I could say was, "Well, you didn't do a bad job of growing up yourself."

I still don't know if I fell in love with his good looks or the uniform. It must have been both because I couldn't keep my eyes off of him. Dan and his cousin talked about old times. When Dan learned there was a dance on Saturday night in one of the little towns out in the country, he asked me if I would go with him. Without hesitating, I agreed.

We saw each other every day that week, and when we went to the dance on Saturday night we had a really great time. The following Monday he said he was going to put some strings on me so I would still be there when he finished Navy Submarine School. I just smiled and said, "Okay." On Thursday he came to the house and gave me a beautiful diamond ring. The following Monday we said our good-byes at the airport and he left for Connecticut to spend three and a half months in Submarine School.

During that period of time I planned our wedding, kept working, and corresponded with Dan by letter every night. On Saturday morning, December 17, 1955, I met Dan's plane in Denver at 7:30 in the morning. Dan's cousin went with me and drove us back to Colorado Springs. Dan and I just looked at each other and talked and kissed. At 7:30 that evening we said our vows to love and care for each other for the rest of our lives.

Now fast forward 50 years. At 7:30 in the evening of Saturday, December 17, 2005 we celebrated 50 years of marriage. Joining us were our four children, fourteen grand-children and three great grandchildren. Many friends and relatives joined us for an evening of dinner, memories, and dancing.

We've had a wonderful life together, even through we were separated many, many years because of Dan's military duties. Now we are retired, in fairly good health, enjoy each others company, and are still in love.

6
ON LEAVE FROM
A TOUR IN VIETNAM

"Cleaving in a Split Second"
Gladys and John

❖ ❖ ❖ ❖ ❖

MY NAME IS GLADYS AND I MET JOHN 36 YEARS ago. I was at a little country bar in our home town with my brother and sister-in-law. While we were there I met John, who was on military leave from a tour in Vietnam.

When he walked in, somehow I knew he was the man for me and I could tell he felt the same way about me. Something we saw in each others eyes created a strange glow that warmed our hearts.

We first met at 1:20 A.M. on Sunday morning April 5. Eleven hours later he asked me to marry him. On Saturday, April 11, we were married. Only seven days had passed since I first met John in the little country bar.

We will always be grateful to our mothers for quickly putting together a big church wedding. With great support from the surrounding community, they were able to fashion a wonderful wedding that even included a huge reception afterwards.

John had been married before and had two children of his own. We had two sons together and now have twelve grandchildren and four great grandchildren. We are just as happy today as we were when we first met thirty-six years ago.

7
NOTES ON THE KITCHEN TABLE

"Cleaving Leaves a Scar"
Jane and Ron
❖ ❖ ❖ ❖ ❖

MY NAME IS JANE. I MET MY HUSBAND, RON, through my boss's secretary at the Panax Corporation where I worked. Her husband worked in the same state office that Ron did. We would dance with each other and we finally started taking dance lessons together. I wouldn't go on a date with him for months. That was foolish, now that I think about it.

We shoved a lifetime into a very short period of time together. He would never hurt me in any way or let anyone else do anything to hurt me. I felt cared for and honored all the time. I think the marriage mold was broken for anyone

I would meet again. Ron and I were very quiet and considerate of each other. We thought and acted like we had just met and were still on a date. Keeping our first date alive was the most fun.

We left notes to each other on the kitchen table. And each day when he came home from work, he could always expect to find me behind the front door with a joke going on ... a very private joke that we could understand. We even joked at the table with facial messages while under the table we continued the joke with our feet. The kids couldn't figure out what we were doing. We made fun of everything.

I think being happy and bouncy and considerate in our relationship should send the message that you can have a good marriage, if you think about the other person as yourself. These few sentences are the best I can do. I don't know what I could add that would explain a rare experience and the happy and sad story of our relationship,

We were only together for five short years. We danced to a life that was cut short with sickness and death. I've been alone since 1985 and I still miss Ron terribly, but I'm left with lots of good memories of the fun we shared. My best advice is, don't expect someone else to make you happy. Learn to be happy within yourself.

8
THEY THOUGHT I WAS A BOY

"Cleaving With a Best Friend"
Pam and Doug

❖ ❖ ❖ ❖ ❖

MY NAME IS PAM. WHEN I WAS VERY YOUNG, MY parents moved away from town to live on a farm owned by my grandfather. A well-known farmer, who lived about 14 miles away, agreed to handle the farming operation with his five sons.

I was nine years old when the boys finished our first spring planting. They decided to play a game of soft ball and invited my brother and me to join them. I wore jeans and a baseball cap, so they thought I was one of the boys until I took my cap off and my blond hair fell to my shoulders. Doug, who was fourteen at the time, remarked, "She is a girl ..."

I saw Doug occasionally but after age eleven, I didn't see him again until my senior year of high school. My date and I were returning home from a formal dinner in nearby Columbus and stopped at a popular pizza place in our town. Suddenly, a blue convertible pulled beside us and two young guys jumped out and clambered into the back seat of my date's car.

I had laid my white spring coat on the back seat to keep it clean. But the two guys plopped themselves down on my coat before I could stop them. One fellow looked at me intently, and then with a smile said he was sorry as he moved my coat. While they were talking I turned facing forward and looked out the window. I was well aware, however, that one of the young men was staring at me. He had a strange sounding voice that somehow seemed familiar.

When they were driving away my date said, "That fellow, Doug, sure stared at you enough. He'll know you the next time he sees you." I asked, "Doug who?" After he explained who Doug was I said, "Oh really! I knew him when I was a young girl. I haven't seen him in years but I knew there was something familiar about his voice."

During the summer after high school graduation, the annual Fourth of July Fish Fry and Carnival opened in the center of town. I was walking down the midway with some girlfriends when a fellow stepped in front of me and said, "Hi, aren't you going to speak?" I thought, "Who are you?" Then something triggered my memory and I knew by his voice that it was Doug. I said, "Hi … sorry but I didn't see you." Later that evening, during fireworks, Doug talked and joked with me as if he knew me well.

A couple of weeks later on Sunday morning, a girlfriend ran up the stairs to my room and said, "Pam, you've got to do me a favor! I'm going picnicking with my boyfriend. Doug is taking his boat and we're all going down to the Ohio River and go water skiing. I asked Doug who he wanted to go with us and he said, 'I want Pam to go.'"

During the day at the River, Doug and I became friends. He became the big brother I didn't have. He would drop by my home from time to time, and I would arrange dates for him with my older girlfriends. We even double dated and during our double dates often Doug would hold my hand or give me a hug, usually as a joke. I thought at times he was serious, but never let myself dwell on it. People in our small town would tell me that Doug liked me and I would laugh and say, "He thinks of me as a kid sister, after all he is almost five years older. Besides, he used to think I was a boy!"

When I came home from school to celebrate my eighteenth, birthday, Doug came to the house with a gift. I don't know how he knew it was my birthday, but he offered to take me to a movie and dinner on Saturday. When I started to pay for my movie ticket, Doug said, "What are you doing? This is a date." I said, "Oh. Right!" and hit him on the shoulder and laughed. But he was dead serious and said, "No! This is a date!" After returning home Doug said, "What would you like to do next weekend?" I asked what he meant and he said, "I mean, let's go out again." I wanted to say no, but I didn't. Doug and I liked the same things and we laughed a lot, so I agreed.

I was away at school, so I didn't see Doug for a while. I had started dating again when Doug showed up. This time he did not go away. The Vietnam War was ongoing and Doug was in the Air Force. He also owned a farm and worked for a large manufacturer, so to say the least, he was busy. This time he kept asking me out. I kept telling my Mother that I was not going to date him anymore, even though we enjoyed our time together.

During the football season, Doug and his brother were scouts for the home town high school football team. Doug asked me to go to the games with him, but said to be aware that some of his family would probably believe we were getting married. We would tell them we were not getting married, that we were only friends, and that I was dating other guys. This was our plan but it didn't stop the rumors from flying.

I kept thinking it would be best if I stopped seeing Doug. I decided with the age difference and college coming, I needed to tell Doug we should move on. About two months before my nineteenth birthday, we dated again and as usual, we had a great time. Toward the end of the date I knew I had to tell Doug that although I really liked him, I could not let this go on.

Then, much to my surprise and out of no-where, Doug pulled me close and said, "Pam, either marry me or you will never see me again!" What a twist! I answered, "Well, I thought someday we would get married." I was shocked at what I was saying. Did that come out of my mouth? I didn't know where those words came from. It was as if someone else was talking, not me.

I suddenly realized that I had fallen in love with my best friend and could not imagine life without him! About nine months later, on May 3, 1969, we had a big church wedding with all the trimmings. Doug always tells me, "I'll never promise you anything, but our lives will not be boring." Boy, what an understatement.

We've been married nearly 37 years. We've worked hard and played hard. We've had good times and we've faced some hard times, but always together hand in hand. We feel blessed because we are such good friends. Being in love adds the whipped cream with the cherry on top.

COLOPHON

This book was produced using the following processes:

Research and gathering
    Web: MS Explorer 7.0

Printer: Lexmark-Inkjet X75

Writing and manuscript building
    Manuscript preparation: MS Word

Copyediting: Peggy Painter, Tom Neal, Jeff Sumner, Dr. Clark, Ruthie Davidson

Cover Designer: John Morris-Reihl, Art and Technology, http://www.artntech.com

Image: Ann Cummins

Design, typesetting & layout: Martha Williams Nichols, aMuse Productions, productionwoman@yahoo.com

Typefaces:
    Body text: Benguiat, 12 pt
    Headers: ITCBenguiatGothic Bold, 10 pt
    Chapter titles: ITCBenguiatGothic Bold, 18 pt
    Chapter subtitles: ITCBenguiatGothic Bold, 14 pt
    Chapter numbers: ITCBenguiatGothic Bold, 10 pt
    Quotations: ACaslon Regular, 12 pt
    Interior quote: Optima Oblique, 11 pt

Conversion: MS Word to QuarkXPress to PDF using Adobe Acrobat 4.0

Printing: Lightning Source, Inc., La Vergne, TN from PDF

Paper: 55lb offset, 444 PPI, crème white, acid free

Cover: Four color, film lamination, Snell Roundhand, Trajan

Binding: Perfect bound (adhesive, soft-cover)

QUICK ORDER FORM

Email orders: *newbook@cleave2.com*

Fax orders: 1.440.306.0649 Send this form.

Telephone orders: 1.866.740.8812 (toll free)

Have this form and your credit card handy.

Postal orders: CAI Publishing,
807 Black Duck Drive,
Port Orange, FL 32127-4726, USA.
Send this form.

Please send (__) copies of the book, "*Life Is Sexually Transmitted.*" I understand that I may return them for a full refund — for any reason, no questions asked.

Send FREE information on:
( ) Speaking ( ) Coaching ( ) Consulting

Your name: _____

Address: _____

City: _____

State: _____ Zip: _____

Telephone: _____

Email: _____

Sales tax: Please add sales tax at point of delivery for books shipped to Florida addresses.

Shipping by air: US: $4.50 for the first book or disk and $2.50 for each additional product. International: $10.00 for first book or disk and $5.50 for each additional product (estimate).

Payment: ( ) Check ( ) Visa ( ) Discover ( ) Master Card
Card number: _____
Name on card: _____
Expiration Date: _____/_____

See: *http://www.cleave2.com*

www.ingramcontent.com/pod-product-compliance
Lightning Source LLC
Chambersburg PA
CBHW021236090426
42740CB00006B/565